curious about

INDEPENDENCE DAY

BY AMY HOUTS

AMICUS LEARNING

What are you

CHAPTER TWO

The History of Independence Day
PAGE **10**

CHAPTER ONE

A Summer Celebration
PAGE **4**

curious about?

CHAPTER THREE

Let's Celebrate!
PAGE **14**

Stay Curious! Learn More . . . 22
Glossary 24
Index 24

Curious About is published by
Amicus Learning, an imprint of Amicus
P.O. Box 227, Mankato, MN 56002
www.amicuspublishing.us

Copyright © 2026 Amicus.
International copyright reserved in all countries.
No part of this book may be reproduced in any
form without written permission from the publisher.

Editor: Ana Brauer
Series Designer: Kathleen Petelinsek
Book Designer and Photo Researcher: Sara Hood

Library of Congress Cataloging-in-Publication Data
Names: Houts, Amy, 1957–author
Title: Curious about Independence Day / Amy Houts.
Description: Mankato, MN : Amicus Learning, 2026. | Series: Curious about holidays | Includes bibliographical references and index. | Audience: Ages 6–9 | Audience: Grades 2–3 | Summary: "Discover the excitement of the Fourth of July! Learn about Independence Day's history, significance, and celebrations in this question-and-answer book for elementary-aged readers. Includes table of contents, glossary, further resources, and index"—Provided by publisher.
Identifiers: LCCN 2025014058 (print) | LCCN 2025014059 (ebook) | ISBN 9798892008464 library binding | ISBN 9798892009126 paperback | ISBN 9798892009782 ebook
Subjects: LCSH: Fourth of July—Juvenile literature
Classification: LCC E286 .A1364 2026 (print) | LCC E286 (ebook) | DDC 394.2634—dc23/eng/20250509
LC record available at https://lccn.loc.gov/2025014058
LC ebook record available at https://lccn.loc.gov/2025014059

Photo Credits: Alamy Stock Photo/Gary Conner, 18, Peter Bennett, 13; Getty Images/Ariel Skelley, 2, 3, 5, 6–7, 15 (second from top), 20–21, FOTOGRAFIA INC., 15 (top), Olena Malik, 15 (middle), Oliver Rossi, 15 (bottom), Pete Saloutos, 16–17, Richard Lautens, 19, SimpleImages, 14; mapsvg.com/CC BY 4.0, 9; Shutterstock/Goinyk Production, 15 (second from bottom), UbjsP, cover, 1; The Noun Project/Made x Made, 22, 23, Muhammad Ikraam, 22, 23; Wikimedia Commons/John Trumbull, 2, 9, 10, public domain, 11

Every effort has been made to contact copyright holders for material reproduced in this book. Any omissions will be rectified in subsequent printings if notice is given to the publisher.

Printed in United States of America

CHAPTER ONE

A SUMMER HOLIDAY

What is Independence Day?

Independence Day is a summer holiday. It is celebrated on July 4. Independence Day is like a birthday party. But it's not for a person. It's for a **nation**. The new nation was the United States of America.

DID YOU KNOW?
Independence Day is also called the Fourth of July.

Independence Day honors the day the US became a country.

A SUMMER HOLIDAY

Who celebrates Independence Day?

A SUMMER HOLIDAY

Many people walk and wave flags in Independence Day parades.

People all across the United States. People from all backgrounds celebrate. All ages take part in the celebration. You can take part, too! The Fourth of July is a time to come together and show pride in the country.

Why do people celebrate Independence Day?

The United States used to be the United **Colonies**. The colonies were part of Great Britain. But people wanted to start their own country. So, they began fighting the Revolutionary War in 1775. The United Colonies became the United States in 1776. Americans celebrate their independence from Great Britain.

DID YOU KNOW?
The United States started with 13 colonies.

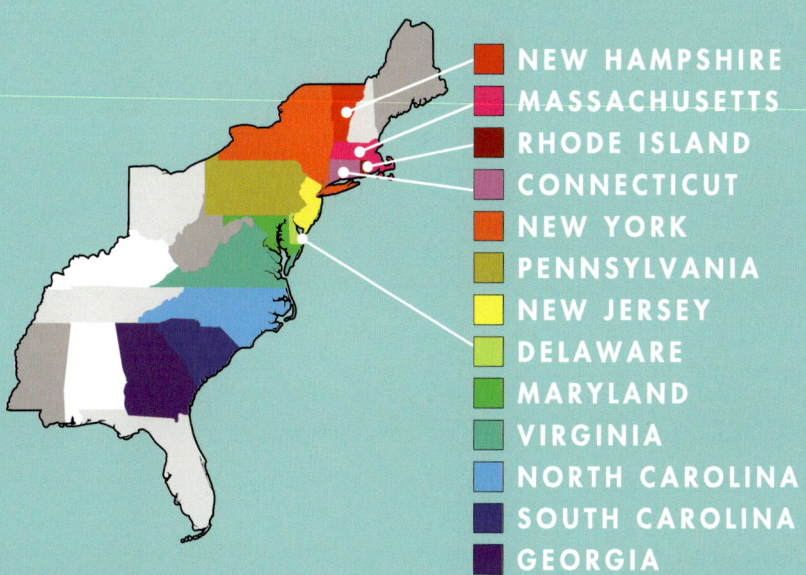

- NEW HAMPSHIRE
- MASSACHUSETTS
- RHODE ISLAND
- CONNECTICUT
- NEW YORK
- PENNSYLVANIA
- NEW JERSEY
- DELAWARE
- MARYLAND
- VIRGINIA
- NORTH CAROLINA
- SOUTH CAROLINA
- GEORGIA

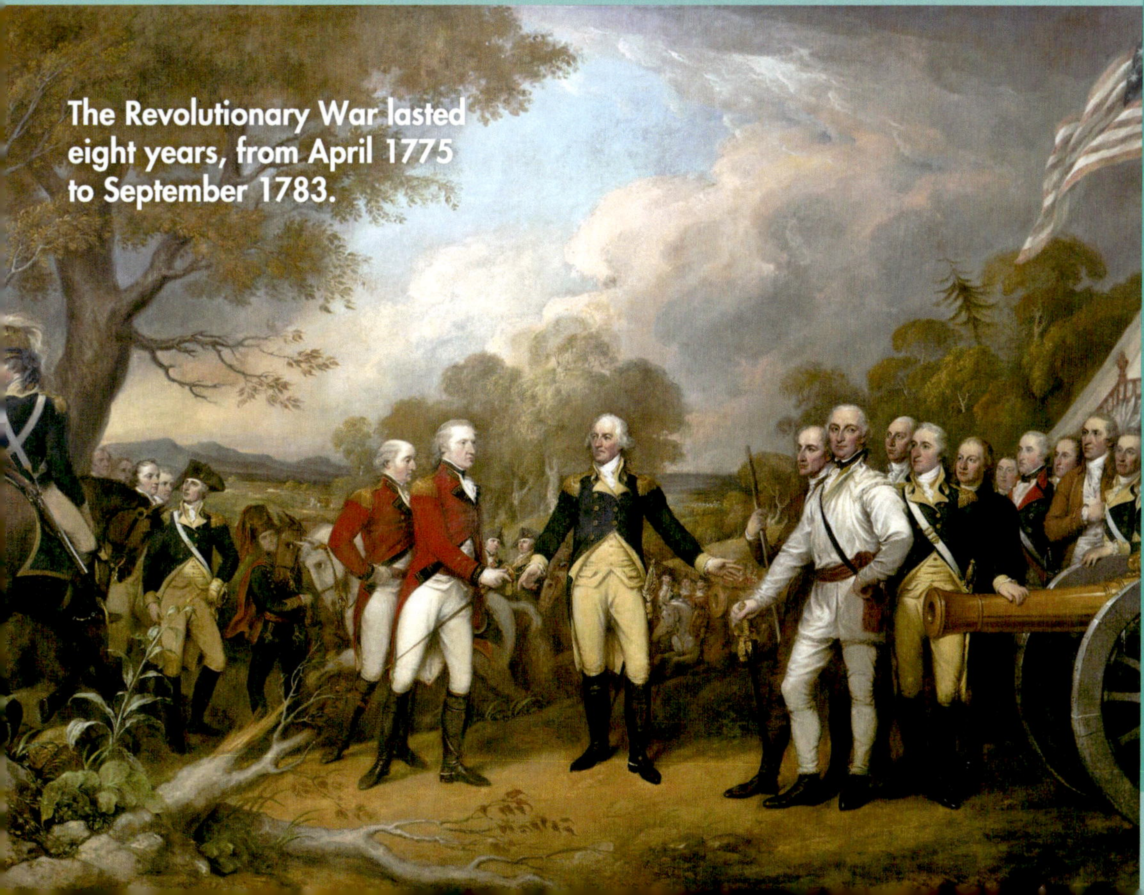

The Revolutionary War lasted eight years, from April 1775 to September 1783.

A SUMMER HOLIDAY

CHAPTER TWO

How long has Independence Day been celebrated?

The Declaration of Independence said that the colonies wanted to be free from Great Britain.

It has been celebrated for about 250 years. On July 4, 1777, there were bonfires. Americans rang bells. They even set off fireworks! That was one year after the government **adopted** the Declaration of Independence. Independence Day became a **national holiday** in 1870.

THE HISTORY OF INDEPENDENCE DAY

THE SIGNERS
56 people signed the Declaration of Independence.

Edward Rutledge was the youngest, age 26.

John Hancock has the biggest signature.

Benjamin Franklin was the oldest, age 70.

When is Independence Day?

Independence Day is July 4. It's always on the same date. That means it falls on different days of the week. Many people have the day off work. What if July 4 falls on a Saturday or Sunday? Then some people don't have to work on Monday.

Many offices and stores close so workers can join in the fun.

THE HISTORY OF INDEPENDENCE DAY

CHAPTER THREE

What do people do on Independence Day?

People wave flags on the Fourth of July to show they love their country.

People wear red, white, and blue. They display an American flag. People spend time with their family. Many people cook outside on July 4. They eat outside, too. People cook burgers and hotdogs. They go to parades. They watch fireworks displays.

COOKOUTS

PARADES

FIREWORKS

BOATING

CAMPING

POPULAR JULY 4 ACTIVITIES

15

Why do people display fireworks on Independence Day?

To celebrate the country's birthday and freedom! In 1777, founding father John Adams said America's birthday should be celebrated with fireworks. Today, fireworks still light up the night sky every Fourth of July.

LET'S CELEBRATE!

DID YOU KNOW?
Fireworks came from China more than 2,000 years ago.

People all over the country light fireworks after dark.

Folk dancers perform in parades for Mexico's Independence Day.

Do other countries have an Independence Day?

Yes, many countries celebrate their independence. Mexico was a colony of Spain. The people called for independence on September 16, 1810. Mexico fought Spain for their freedom. Canada became a country on July 1, 1867. Their holiday is called Canada Day.

Canada Day is also celebrated with big parades.

LET'S CELEBRATE!

DID YOU KNOW?
Canada was not independent from Great Britain until 1982.

Are fireworks safe for kids?

LET'S CELEBRATE!

Safe celebrations help everyone have fun and avoid injuries on the Fourth of July.

No, fireworks are not safe for kids. You can get hurt. Leave it to an adult. But you can celebrate in other ways. Wave a flag or glow stick. Pop a confetti popper. Twirl a ribbon streamer. Have fun and be safe!

STAY CURIOUS!

ASK MORE QUESTIONS

Where are the biggest July 4 fireworks displays in the U.S.?

Why do we have parades on Independence Day?

Try a BIG QUESTION: What does freedom mean?

SEARCH FOR ANSWERS

Search the library catalog or the Internet.
A librarian, teacher, or parent can help you.

Using Keywords
Find the looking glass.

🔍

Keywords are the most important words in your question.

❓

If you want to know about:
- big fireworks displays, type: BIGGEST JULY 4 FIREWORKS
- why we have parades on Independence Day, type: HISTORY OF JULY 4 PARADES

LEARN MORE

FIND GOOD SOURCES

Here are some good, safe sources you can use in your research. Your librarian can help you find more.

Books

Make Your Own Independence Day Crafts by Kayla Rossow, 2025.

20 Fun Facts About Independence Day by Katie Kawa, 2025.

Internet Sites

Kiddle | Fireworks facts for kids
https://kids.kiddle.co/Firework
Kiddle is an online encyclopedia for kids. Learn more about fireworks.

National Geographic Kids | Independence Day
https://kids.nationalgeographic.com/history/article/independence-day
This site has information about Independence Day and more.

Every effort has been made to ensure that these websites are appropriate for children. However, because of the nature of the Internet, it is impossible to guarantee that these sites will remain active indefinitely or that their contents will not be altered.

SHARE AND TAKE ACTION

Make a red, white, and blue dessert.
Ask a guardian to help you top a cake with white frosting, strawberries, and blueberries.

Watch an Independence Day parade.
Ask a trusted adult to take you to a parade or watch one on TV.

See a fireworks display.
Ask an adult to take you to see fireworks.

GLOSSARY

adopted Approved and officially accepted.

colony A group of people from one country settling in another country.

independence Being free from outside control.

nation A people living in the same region of the world and having a common history, language, and culture.

national holiday A holiday that is celebrated throughout a country.

INDEX

Adams, John, 16
Americans, 8, 11, 14
Canada, 18, 19
colonies, 8, 9, 10
Declaration of Independence, 10, 11
fireworks, 11, 14, 16–17, 21
flags, 6, 14, 21
Fourth of July, 4, 7, 14, 16, 20
freedom, 16, 18
Great Britain, 8, 10, 19
parades, 6, 14, 18, 19
Revolutionary War, 8, 9

About the Author

Amy Houts celebrates Independence Day with food and fun. Her family grills hamburgers and watches fireworks. Amy is the author of more than 100 picture books. When Amy is not writing, you can find her walking her dog in Northwest Missouri.